BEEKEEPING
FOR BEGINNERS

The New Complete Guide to Raise a Healthy and Thriving Beehive.
How to Use Top Bar Hives, Take Care of Your Colony and Harvest
Honey Insider Tips on Working With Beeswax

Shawn Baxter

TABLE OF CONTENTS

USEFUL BEEKEEPING TERMS

In this guide, you'll find some beekeeping jargon that you may not be familiar with. When these come up, we'll do our best to explain them as clearly as we can, but we're making this list here as a quick reference guide to make navigating this book a little easier.

- **Absconding**: when bees abandon a hive
- **Apiary**: a place where bees are raised
- **Bearding**: an action performed by bees in hot weather where they gather outside the hive entrance (in a beard-like shape). The purpose is to create more space inside the hive to ventilate it and reduce the temperature/humidity.
- **Brood**: refers to the larvae, pupae, and eggs of honeybees

- **Burr Comb:** a type of honeycomb bees build when there is excessive bee space in the hive. The Burr comb is constructed randomly, so it looks a little messy. It can be a nuisance for taking apart and maintaining the hive, as it glues hive parts together.

- **Capped Honey:** when a cell has been filled with honey, it gets sealed with wax ("capped") which prevents the honey from drying out.

- **Drawing Comb:** the act of constructing a honeycomb performed by worker bees.

- **Fanning:** an action performed by bees where they fan their wings to cool down the hive.

- **Foundation:** A foundation is a pressed wax or plastic frame insert with a hexagonal template on which bees will build their comb.

- **Green Honey:** green honey comes from honey that is "uncapped," so it is not ready for harvest. It has a high moisture content so it can be very high in yeast. It's super gooey, doesn't taste great, and isn't safe to consume.

- **Honey Supers:** the layers where honey is stored and collected in the hive. Super is short for "superstructure."

- **Nucleus Box:** a wooden box that contains around 3 or 5 frames. Basically, a mini beehive is often used to populate a new hive.

- **Robbing:** when bees from one hive infiltrate another and steal the stored honey.

- **Swarm:** a group of bees (including a queen) that has left the hive (usually because the queen was replaced) and has settled in another nearby location. Capturing a swarm is a way to populate a new hive.

- **Queen Excluder:** a layer in the beehive that worker bees can pass through, but queens or drone bees cannot. This layer prevents the queen from laying eggs in the honey supers of a hive.

INTRODUCTION TO BEEKEEPING

"The Beekeeper must first of all be a bee lover,
or he will never succeed"- Ticknor Edwardes

Beekeeping is the perfect hobby for anyone who enjoys the great outdoors, wants to learn a new skill, has some free time, and maybe has some land they want to put to good use. It's a hobby, or sometimes even a source of livelihood, that can bring great joy to those involved. Every step of the beekeeping process (from setting up your hives to harvesting the honey) can be done by both pros and amateurs; it's just essential to learn the basics first because beekeeping is much harder and more technical than it may seem.

This guide will cover many of the key aspects of starting your new hive, taking care of your bees, harvesting honey, etc. There's plenty to cover, and it may be a little overwhelming if you're a first-time beekeeper. But, like all things, the most important thing is to enjoy the process! Beekeeping is a fantastic source of relaxation for many, as it can be incredibly satisfying and therapeutic- similar to growing vegetables or flowers.

So if you're looking to become a beekeeper, for a hobby or otherwise, you're in the right place.

In this introduction, we're going to cover some of the backgrounds of beekeeping itself, its origins and history, and several reasons why people start doing it. To get straight into the details of how to get started, skip ahead to chapter 2 for an introduction to the beehive itself.

Let's get started!

CHAPTER 1

The History of Beekeeping

The Beginning

As far as the origins of beekeeping go, historians tend to disagree on when *exactly* beekeeping started. Like most things in history, it's tough to pinpoint an exact time and place. Some say it was 9000 years ago, and some settle closer to 10,000 years ago. But the point is **beekeeping has been around for a while**. Our ancestors have been farming bees and harvesting honey since prehistoric times, so this is a practice that is firmly rooted in our history.

These numbers come from artifacts that historians have collected depicting images of beekeeping or items found with traces of honeycomb on them. For example, pottery from Prehistoric Europe was found with traces of honeycomb and cave drawings depicting bee farming in countless locations; Asia, Australia, Southern Africa, and Europe.

Whether they were farming bees to collect honey for consumption or medical purposes, beekeeping was a significant part of farming culture. This significance has continued into modern times, and bees have played a large part in shaping agriculture, society, and human traditions.

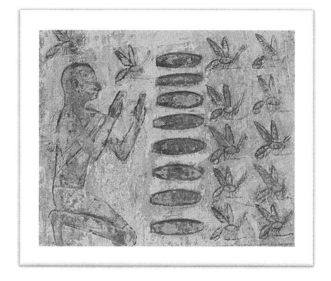

One of the first depictions of beekeeping was discovered from a drawing inside a cave close to Valencia, Spain. It's thought that this drawing is from the Mesolithic Age (the Stone Age), around 10,000-8,000 BC. The picture shows a woman farming honey from a beehive perched on the side of a cliff. The woman is also drawn, surrounded by several bees buzzing around. Not only does this picture give evidence of bee farming being practiced at this time, but it also gives us a good idea of the farming methods people used to use. As mentioned, the bee nest is shown on a cliff face, with the woman climbing a rope ladder to reach it. Naturally, this is where many beehives tend to be found (high up in trees or hidden in the cracks of rock faces). While incredibly dangerous due to the sheer height of these hives, this is a method of honey harvesting that is still practiced widely in certain parts of the world. Tribes in the Syrian desert, as well as groups of people in Nepal and Sri Lanka, are known to do this. For these people, collecting wild honey is an essential part of their culture and rituals and a key source of income and nourishment.

The Origins of Organized Beekeeping

Of course, we would not recommend climbing up huge rock faces with a rope ladder to gather honey. This guide is focused purely on the practice of *organized beekeeping,* A.K.A., and the establishment and running of beehives in a way that simulates a natural environment and ensures safety and efficiency for your honeybees. There are quite a few known accounts of societies that practiced this type of beekeeping, but we're going to stick to discussing the Ancient Egyptians and Ancient Mayans.

Beekeeping from the Ancient Egyptians

The earliest evidence of organized beekeeping is from Ancient Egypt. Beekeepers at this time would use hives constructed from twigs and reeds, which homed colonies of a species of bee known now as the Egyptian Honeybee. By 1500 BCE, beekeeping was a popular practice across most of Egypt, and honey became so valuable that farmers would use it as currency. Beekeepers collected their honey in clay pots and labeled it according to its color and quality.

Honey and beeswax played a lot of important roles in Ancient Egyptian society. Honey was a common food source but was also used for a plethora of religious and medical reasons. Even today, honey is hailed as a fantastic makeshift antiseptic for wounds, and the Ancient Egyptians often used it in the exact same way. Honey was also a common sacrificial offering to Egyptian Gods, and honey pots were commonly left in tombs for the deceased to carry into the afterlife.

Beeswax was often used to make objects like candles and was a substance used in the process of mummification. According to legend, the Egyptian God Ra (God of the Sun) was thought to produce tears that would turn into bees, and these bees would bring fertility by pollinating all of the flowers along the Nile.

So beekeeping held a lot of significance in this ancient society, both practically and spiritually.

Beekeeping from the Ancient Mayans

The Mayans are a group that has been around for a long time and was thought to be extremely knowledgeable about beekeeping. Along with many other skills they developed concerning keeping bees, they were known to be really efficient with their farms- often splitting their existing hives to increase honey yield and increase the bee populations of each hive. They also knew the harm in over-harvesting a single hive and realized the importance of leaving honey remaining for the bees to feed on in the winter. Several Spanish accounts discussing the Mayans and their beekeeping accolades exist, and they mention how they had very well-developed apiaries (bee farms) that housed hundreds, and sometimes thousands, of native Stingless Honeybees. This species is native to Mesoamerica, but the population has sadly plummeted more than 90% over the last two decades due to deforestation.

The Mayans used materials such as hollowed-out logs for their hives. Often these hives were carved in some way, including figures and ornaments that signified who the hive owner was.

Each hive was designed with a simple hole in the center, where the bees could enter and exit, and a hole at each end plugged with stoppers fashioned from small stone discs. Several of these discs have since been found and are the earliest known beekeeping-related artifacts to exist, dating from 300 BCE to 300 CE.

Beekeeping During the Middle Ages (European) and Colonial Periods

For the most part, medieval beekeeping practices in Europe were inspired largely by early methods- farmers would seek large trees that housed wild native honey bee nests. After locating a nest, the beekeeper would fashion protective panels

of wood from other parts of the tree. These panels were used to protect the nest from damage due to weather or predators. These keepers often also cut off the tops of trees to prevent them from getting too tall, making the nest more accessible and less of a perilous endeavor.

This practice of using trees to farm bees led to the creation of what was called Bee Forests throughout northern Europe- a lot of which were owned by either the Church or aristocrats.

These bee forests contributed largely to local European economies, so they were widely beneficial, but the biggest disadvantage of this method was that it was not at all time-efficient.

At the same time, parts of eastern Europe were using vessels such as hollowed-out logs and basket-woven vessels as beehives. Areas predominantly using these included regions of Poland, Germany, and Lithuania. These beekeeping methods were beneficial in many ways, but mainly because the hives could be easily transported and stored much closer to human settlements, making harvesting and maintenance a lot more convenient for the beekeepers.

Britain, France, and some parts of western Europe were fashioning beehives from stones, creating stone hives called "bee boles." They were often located on the south- or southeast-facing walls and close to orchards and gardens to protect the hives from bad weather conditions.

During the colonial period, shortly after the "discovery" of America, ship cargo records tell us how European Honeybees were one of the first animals to be shipped alongside early settlers. Bees were considered precious cargo at this time, as they could provide honey, beeswax, and pollinate crops. During this time, honey was often recognized as a currency in place of sugar (which was highly taxed by the English). Due to this, they were not only a useful honey and beeswax useful commodity but also an essential source of income for many. Honey and beeswax were used as key ingredients in producing several products; candles, shoe polish, lipstick, and mead. The importation of bees to North America led to honeybees spreading across many regions.

Beekeeping in Modern Times

Even though wild beekeeping is still practiced in certain societies, a large majority of honey is now collected via organized bee farms. These days, the most common set-up for beehives is the Langstroth hive: consisting of wooden boxes containing wooden frames which can be removed individually to harvest the honey and wax with ease, as well as allowing easy inspection of the hive's condition. This hive structure is also good for transportation, so it is widely considered to be the most beneficial hive structure choice for commercial or large-scale beekeeping. Moving hives is a common practice by modern beekeepers to allow the bees to be put closer to the best foraging areas and near flowers with the highest nectar yields depending on the season.

Within Europe, beekeepers often move their hives into the countryside later in the growing season. In the UK, this is when the heather is in full bloom, and in France, when the lavender is blooming. Moving hives near these types of flowers creates a yield of honey that is extra special and much more valuable- so migrating the hives may be a little hassle but is well worth it in the end.

In the US, migrating bee hives is, without a doubt, the most profitable way to make money through beekeeping. During the main growing season, hundreds of thousands of hives are transported down highways on large trucks to massive fruit, nut, and berry farms. Beekeepers often utilize bees to pollinate crops, such as almonds, alfalfa, oranges, and berries, to maximize crop yields. Due to the immense scale of these farms, it's not enough to rely on local honey bees to pollinate these crops, so bees are brought in from other places to offer a helping hand. Overall these operations are highly profitable, but there is controversy surrounding it concerning how the practice can threaten the health and well-being of the honeybees, as well as other pollinating species.

To overcome the threats that wildlife may face in these cases is to support local beekeepers and organic agriculture as much as you possibly can.

CHAPTER 2

Why Do Beekeeping?

Now that we've covered the **extensive** history of beekeeping, let's look at all the reasons for actually doing it yourself. In this section, we'll look at all kinds of benefits gained from beekeeping and some reasons people may choose this lifestyle. If you're still on the fence about whether to start this hobby or you're looking for another reason to get into it, this section is for you!

Benefits of Beekeeping

There are **countless** advantages that beekeeping can bring to your garden, as well as your general well-being. Explore a few here, and perhaps you'll learn a few things that you didn't know previously.

1. It's Fascinating
2. It Doesn't Break the Bank as Much as you May Think
3. It's Good for the Environment
4. The Plethora of Benefits of Honey
5. It's Incredibly Therapeutic
6. It's Great for Kids
7. It Helps the Local Economy

8. Bees can be Put Anywhere

9. It Helps You Connect to Your Community

10. You Won't Just Get Honey

11. You Could Get a Tax Break

Let's look at each of these benefits in a little more detail!

It's Fascinating

Bee enthusiasts absolutely undoubtedly believe that beekeeping is an incredibly interesting subject to learn! The reason for this is probably because there is a lot more to bees than people may think. Bees establish societies with complex structures, roles, and conventions that are really fascinating to both study and observe. Even the methods that bees use to communicate are interesting. And like most things, it's far better to learn it through seeing it with your own eyes than simply reading it on a website or in a textbook.

Due to bees' integral role in our ecosystems overall, keeping bees will also bring you a new appreciation for nature. A bee has probably pollinated every tree or flower you see, and studying beekeeping will make that fact far more significant.

These are things that everyday people never pay attention to, but they will be in the forefront of your mind as an active beekeeper. Fascinating, no?

It Doesn't Break the Bank as Much as you May Think

When considering whether to start a hobby like this, it's natural to worry about how much it'll cost you. It's a hobby that takes up a lot of time and requires a lot of equipment- it has to cost a small fortune, right?

Well...not really.

The main reason beekeeping is not that expensive is due to the fact that **it's a hobby that can pay for itself.** Don't forget that with beekeeping, you're producing products as well as having a great time. With some networking and contacts, these products can easily be sold. So, if anything, the money you put into building that new hive **can be seen as an investment** because you'll get something back out of it eventually.

At the end of the day, the basic equipment you'll require to start up a bee colony (the clothing, the hives, the bees etc.) will probably put you back around 500 dollars. Which is still a little expensive, but compare that to all the money you might have to spend on hobbies such as golf, scuba diving, and mountain climbing. These hobbies involve a load of expensive specialized equipment, probably some kind of private tutoring, maybe a membership, or some kind of qualification. It all adds up! So beekeeping is a lot cheaper than the alternatives- and is a good way to earn money back.

Also, if you're looking into getting bees because you want to dip your toes in the game of raising livestock, starting a beehive is definitely one of the cheaper options. Raising livestock like pigs or cows costs A LOT more; everything from feed to medical fees to the space required.

So beekeeping is a great introductory choice.

It's Good for the Environment

In this day and age, finding ways to help the environment is something everyone is looking into. But apart from recycling your plastics appropriately, and cutting down on your water usage, the ways that humans can

actually make a large impact on the environmental crisis is sadly quite limited.

However, keeping bees is a great way to positively impact the environment. Bees transfer pollen from one plant to another, which fertilizes them and helps them grow. Professionals estimate that *bees contribute to around 30% of the world's food production. 90% of wild plants rely on bees and other pollinators to survive.* It was

Albert Einstein who said that *human beings would last a mere 4 years if bees were to go extinct.* So it's fair to say that bees significantly impact our planet. The best way to make a positive difference is to help bees survive and thrive as much as possible; A.K.A, **give them a safe and prosperous home!** Even if your primary purpose for raising bees is income, you can rest well knowing that you're contributing to something greater alongside making an honest living.

The Plethora of Benefits of Honey

It's no secret that honey is **somewhat of a miracle ingredient.** For centuries it's been hailed as liquid gold, with countless antiseptic and healing properties. It's a great source of antioxidants that can help with inflammation and digestive issues.

Some people claim that eating honey in small amounts daily can immunize you from allergies. It's also claimed to be fantastic at healing a sore throat- stirring a spoonful of honey into a steaming cup of ginger tea can do wonders.

Due to its natural antibacterial and antimicrobial properties, it's also been used since ancient times as a treatment for wounds. Others claim it can help boost memory when consumed regularly.

Honey is also a common ingredient in skincare and haircare products due to its moisturizing properties. Some people use it on their hair directly as a scalp treatment for issues such as dandruff, and it's a popular addition to many homemade face mask recipes.

As well as all the above, eating honey is generally great for you! Honey is a natural sweetener that is much healthier than refined sugar and has a delicious flavor. It's also packed with nutrients like iron, manganese, riboflavin, and niacin. If you buy honey from a supermarket, it's likely to have been pasteurized, which involves heating the honey, so it gets stripped of a bunch of the aforementioned naturally-present nutrients. Plus, when it comes to flavor, there is **nothing better than pure stuff.** Ask any beekeeper, and they'll tell you the exact same. **Even the first batch of honey you produce will be much better than anything store-bought.**

Plus, the type of flower the bees collect their pollen from when making your honey affects the flavor- that's why you see honey labeled as "wildflower honey" or "lavender honey." If you put your beehives closer to certain flower types, you'll get honey that can have an incredible and unique flavor. It's a great chance to experiment.

It's Incredibly Therapeutic

Is there anything more calming after a long day's work than going out into your garden and spending some time in nature? Tending to your beehive can have the same soothing effect that you would get from doing a spot of gardening or walking through a beautiful meadow. Plus, with beekeeping, like gardening, you'll get that great feeling that you're doing something constructive- so **not only will beekeeping keep you relaxed and calm, but it's a great way to motivate yourself** if you have a long to-do list to tackle.

For someone who is not familiar with beekeeping, the idea that this hobby can be relaxing might be a bit of a surprise; after all, it involves interacting with hundreds of insects that could sting you if you make a wrong move. But *if you've done beekeeping before, you'll know that all it takes is the correct equipment and method, and it's the most relaxing way you can spend your time!*

It's Great for Kids

Now, of course, it's not recommended to just throw your kids at your beehives and hope for the best. A child that is anywhere near your bees **must be supervised at all times.** But the nature of beekeeping should not limit children's involvement in the hobby- this is an activity that *can be super rewarding for all ages!*

Beekeeping is a great thing to get kids involved in because it **provides opportunities to learn about the natural life cycles in their local environment.** It's also great for teaching children

how to value and appreciate nature more and demonstrating to them how we can take care of it (as well as why we should!).

If you don't have kids of your own, why not reach out to kids in your close or distant family to host an activity day? Or even reach out to local schools, garden clubs, or youth groups to organize some kind of talk where you show children all the joy and excitement beekeeping involves! This is a great way to give back to the local community via your hobby also.

It Helps the Local Economy

It's predicted that in America alone, a *staggering 15 billion dollars worth of crops are pollinated each year thanks to bees.* All kinds of crops grown in the US, everything from apples to cucumbers, have bees to thank for their plentiful harvest yields. Plus, *the honey that bees produce in the US is estimated to be worth around 150 million dollars.*

So, naturally, this means that fewer bees will mean fewer crops. Fewer crops will mean higher production costs, eventually resulting in higher prices for produce. So **more bees will help to keep the prices the everyday person pays for their groceries a little lower.** Every little helps, after all.

Bees can be Put Anywhere

Apart from concerns about safety, money, or time, one of the main reasons an individual may be hesitant about getting into beekeeping is concerns about space. A beehive must require a large amount of open space and should be as far away from buildings as possible, right?

Wrong.

Firstly, bees are incredibly quiet when inside their hive and are very unlikely to bother you if put close to a building. Actually, they can fit quite comfortably next to a farmhouse or a wall or even on the roof of a building without causing any disturbances.

Concerning space, beehives are not as big as you may think. A **standard beehive will be around 20 by 16 inches,** so it fits within a few square feet. If you have one or two, you can fit them on any piece of land you've got going.

When considering the practicality of owning a beehive, it's a hobby that *doesn't need to take up much time if you don't have the time to spare.* Bees are independent creatures, so they don't require much TLC overall. Bees will happily soldier on with around 30 minutes of maintenance from you weekly, plus a little additional time each year to extract your honey. So if you're stopping yourself from getting into beekeeping because you have a full-time job and don't have much time to dedicate, that wouldn't be an issue!

It Helps You Connect to Your Community

You're highly likely to have some kind of local beekeeping association within driving distance of you, which will hold events and meetings every now and then. Getting involved in

organizations like this is *a great way to make new friends, learn more about the topic, and share your passion with others in your community.*

People new to beekeeping are often surprised by how many people around them are involved in the hobby, so why not try to talk with a stranger at a party about it and find out if they know anyone involved in it also?

You Won't Just Get Honey

We've covered many benefits of beekeeping so far, and the biggest one is probably the honey you can get out of it for consumption or profit. But it's not just honey that you can gain from beekeeping.

In fact, beehives can churn out a whole load of incredible things, including **beeswax, propolis, pollen, honeycomb, and royal jelly.**

Some of these may be familiar to you, but others may be completely alien. Some are food products, others are often used in products such as candles or cosmetics, and most have incredible medical benefits.

Royal jelly, for example, is an ingredient known to have various health benefits, including anti-aging and wound healing properties. It's often used as an ingredient in anti-aging skincare.

Propolis is also a wonderful ingredient known for helping people deal with allergies, as well as solving a lot of various skin or digestive issues.

So the things your beehive will produce are rather varied in nature, but pretty much *all of them are hailed as some form of superfood!* Knowing how to harvest each of these ingredients will require a little more dedicated research, but it will be well worth it. **We'll just touch on how to harvest honey and beeswax in this book.**

You Could get a Tax Break

So one of the main reasons one might get into beekeeping is as a way to earn income. If you're making money from your beehives, then it counts as a business- no matter how big or small. If you're only caring for your bees and selling their honey a few times a month, that still counts as income, which means *all of the equipment you buy for your business will be expenses when filing your annual tax returns.* The tools you'll need to start will add up to a small amount, so knowing that you can claim them as expenses might bring you a little peace of mind.

If you're unsure about the exact tax situation regarding where you live, be sure to book an appointment with an accountant or tax advisor to discuss it.

CHAPTER 3

What Do You Need to Get Started?

"Good beekeepers have sticky hive tools and
smell like smoke": Marina Marchese

Now we've covered the background of beekeeping and some of the biggest benefits of getting stuck into this hobby; it's time to look at what you'll actually need!

As you can imagine, a few key pieces of kit **are necessary to set up and maintain a beehive**-some you may know, and others you may not. We'll cover a comprehensive list of the basics and a bit of background info about each one.

Let's get started!

The basic equipment beekeeping requires as follows:

- A Hive
- A Hive Tool
- A Smoker
- Protective Clothing with a Hat & Veil
- Gloves
- Bee Brush
- Feeders

Look at each item in more detail below.

A Hive

Obviously, one of the most crucial pieces of equipment for housing a bee colony is an actual beehive that your little friends can call their home. We'll talk more about beehives later, including a step-by-step guide in chapter 4 that will show you how to build your very own top-bar hive.

If you weren't aware, hives are a little more complicated than just a wooden box that houses bees; their design involves many different parts and layers to help maximize the efficient harvesting of the bee's products. The hive itself includes everything from the internal "nest" area, honey supers (where excess honey is produced, stored, and harvested by you), an outer cover to protect the hive from bad weather conditions, and a hive stands to keep the bottom of the hive dry and insulated.

A Hive Tool

Hive tools are basically a kind of metal stick. You can get ones that are flat but can also get metal ones that are curved at the end, but they all serve a similar purpose. This little stick is super handy for all kinds of reasons, but the main one is that it allows you to **pry the hive open**. Inside your beehive, you'll

find that your bees use a material called propolis to stick everything together, and it's basically a resin-type glue. The hive tool **allows you to open the hive, scrap propolis from places, detach comb from the sides of the hive, detach frames,** etc. It's incredibly useful.

Smoker

Having a smoker at the ready when working with bees is really crucial. Releasing smoke in and around the hive **helps to calm your bees and make them generally more docile** before you open your hive up and go digging around. Basically, the way that this works is that the smoke causes the bees to eat more honey, as they are tricked into thinking there is a potential fire threat nearby, and **having a full stomach makes them much calmer and less likely to sting you.**

When a beehive faces a potential danger of any kind, the "guard bees" move into action and release a kind of alarm pheromone to warn the rest of the colony. This pheromone smells a lot like bananas, so if you smell this while you're close to your hive, it's probably a good idea to release more smoke to mask it. *Due to this, it's not generally recommended for beekeepers to eat bananas right before tending to their hive, as the bees in the hive might detect the smell and get distressed.*

Regarding what fuel to use for your smoker, some common choices are **grass, pine straw, or burlap.**

Protective Clothing (with a hat & veil)

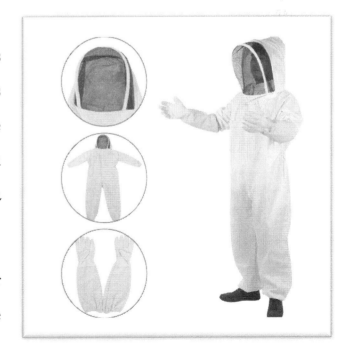

Now, there are people who tend to their beehives without any form of protective gear. While this might be comfortable for those more experienced, there is absolutely no shame in opting to wear protective gear. And **if you're a beginner, it's definitely recommended to wear it.**

It should be emphasized that the protective gear you select **should** include some kind of face protection because bees tend to go for the face when defending themselves.

Because bees can detect carbon dioxide being released, they tend to react aggressively when mammals breathe out heavily (as they might do if nervous or tired). Bees can't sense fear, as people often believe, but **they can sense fear-related behavior, such as heavy breathing.** So if you don't feel 100% comfortable around your bees, **it's best to keep your face completely covered and protected.**

Even if you don't want to purchase a full-body astronaut-looking type suit, at least protect your head, face, and hands.

Gloves

As we just mentioned in the above point, protecting your hands is just as important as protecting your face for several reasons. The main reason you want to keep your hands covered is that while bees can detect nervous behavior through breathing, **they can also detect nervousness through shaky hands.** Of course, navigating your way around a beehive is far easier without gloves, so many more experienced beekeepers choose not to wear them, but **it's highly recommended for beginners.**

Regarding gloves for beekeeping, they're usually made of either soft leather or other durable but flexible materials. The material must be tough enough that it can shield you from stings, but it's flexible enough to be practical. They also tend to extend up the arm pretty far (to just below the elbow) to ensure your hands and wrists are fully covered. If you're shopping around for some, it's a good idea to look for gloves with ventilation around the wrists, as this will be a lifesaver if you're tending to your bees on a hot day.

Bee Brush

A bee brush is a useful tool for those moments when you want to gently move your bees off of one comb to a different place. This is necessary for many situations; when you need to harvest your honey, when you need to remove swarms, or repair broken honeycomb, etc. It's a good idea to use the brush only when you absolutely have to, as your bees will really hate it.

Uncapping Knife/Fork/Scratcher

This is a device you'll need when you're harvesting honey. Uncapping is the process of removing wax that forms on top of honey cells in order to remove the honey. An uncapping tool will allow you to harvest honey with one simple swipe.

Feeders

A feeder is a gadget that holds sugar syrup to feed bees throughout the year. This is useful for times when bees need energy, but honey isn't available for some reason. Some feeders are designed to be put at the hive entrance, but some are designed to be placed inside the hive cavity. Alternatively, you could fashion a makeshift feeder by putting sugar syrup in a plastic food bag and cutting a small slit (around 5") in the top of the bag with a razor knife.

CHAPTER 4

Where Do You Get Bees?

Having all of the equipment you need to set up your beehive is great and all, but what about the bees? There are a few different methods you can use to kick-start your colony, and we'll detail a few of the easiest ones below!

Before anything else, we need to answer a crucial question:

When should you populate your beehive?

The best time to populate your beehive is **in the spring.**

Which, depending on whereabouts in the world you're located, **will probably start around April.** However, as beekeeping is a hobby that has recently increased in popularity, we **recommend sourcing your bees as early as January to ensure you start your colony on time.** Sometimes **there is a backlog that can take month**s to get through.

Please keep reading for our recommended methods to populate your beehive.

Honeybee Packages

A *honeybee package* is a box that contains one isolated inseminated queen bee and around 10,000 worker bees. You can get these packages from bee breeders directly, which are good for easily and effectively populating any hive. Due to their ease of use, **these packages tend**

to sell out pretty fast, so make sure you're well-connected to apiaries (places where bees are kept) within your local area to ensure you can source a package when you need to.

If in doubt, a quick google search of "bee packages" should do the trick.

Just make sure the place you're sourcing from is reliable and practices ethical beekeeping.

How to Install a Honey Bee Package

When you receive your bee package, **you'll need to install it within 1 or 2 days.** To install it, first remove the queen from the box (keeping her in her cage). You can remove the queen by first knocking the bee package on the ground to get all the bees to go to the bottom, removing the can of sugar syrup on top, and quickly

grabbing the queen bee cage (which should be attached just next to the syrup tin inside the box), and replacing the sugar syrup can as quickly as possible to avoid your bees escaping. The queen bee cage will be sealed with hard candy, which the bees will chew through to allow the queen to escape. This ritual allows the worker bees time to get used to the queen's scent and makes it less likely that the colony will reject her. It's recommended for you to use a point to make a hole in the candy to get the bees started, but be very careful not to release the bee or damage them while doing this. Place the queen cage at the bottom of the hive cavity if you're working with a top-bar hive (the hive type we will focus on in this guide).

To get the rest of your bees into the hive, tap the package onto the ground one more time to get all the bees away from the top entrance. Remove the sugar syrup can and swiftly dump the bees into the hive. Try to get as many out of the box as possible, gently shaking it from side to side to make it easier. A few stubborn bees will stay in the package, so once you're happy, lean the package's entrance against the beehive entrance and allow them to make their way inside at their own pace.

Put your bars and roof back onto your hive, and you're set!

Extra: It's a good idea to set up some sugar water solution for your bees when installing them into the hive to help them start building honeycomb.

Nucleus Boxes

A nucleus box often referred to as a "nuc," is basically a mini beehive. It's often a wooden box that contains between 3 and 5 frames filled with honey and brood (bee eggs, larvae, pupae), 1 queen bee, and sufficient worker bees to populate/expand a new hive.

Nuc boxes can be bought from apiaries and bee breeders quite easily. If you're choosing between a nucleus box and a bee package as your population strategy, a nuc box might be better, as the bees will already have some eggs, honey stores, and larvae to work with. They'll be able to build up the hive much faster using a nuc box as they won't be starting from square one.

Once you empty your nuc box into your new hive, an empty nuc box is a great option for a makeshift trap for catching swarms (see next section). If you catch a swarm in a nuc box, you'll be able to leave the swarm in it for a while to start to build up honeycomb instead of installing them into a new hive immediately, which just makes the whole process a little easier and less stressful.

Swarming

When it comes to populating beehives, **swarming is the most natural method to use as it utilizes a very naturally-occurring phenomenon.** Swarming occurs when a colony replaces the old queen, and the replaced queen leaves the hive with around half of the hive and some honey. These swarms will land on a structure close to the original hive, and "scout bees" will leave the swarm to find a more suitable location for them to set up their new permanent hive. During this time, the swarm can be captured and put into a new hive to populate it. These swarms can adapt to a new hive easily and will be ready to start building honeycomb pretty much instantly.

Due to the fact that swarms are local to the area they'll be found in; this method is *great for ensuring strong genetics amongst the local bee population.* They'll also *probably fare better than bee colonies that have been transported cross-country* (as bee packages or nuc boxes sometimes

are). This method is also the cheapest way to populate a beehive, as you can easily capture the hive yourself (read below to find out how to).

So while swarming is a great method for populating hives, keep in mind that swarms **have to be naturally found, so they're not a guaranteed source of bees** (like bee packages are).

How to Catch & Install a Swarm

Before doing anything, ensure you have your beekeeping equipment ready. To catch a swarm, you'll need to have the following:

- a cardboard box (or nucleus box)
- a light-colored bed sheet (or tarp)
- pruning shears
- a bee brush
- tape
- protective gear
- lemongrass oil
- a ladder or stool (if necessary)

Catching a Swarm

Once you've found a swarm that you've determined you can **safely capture**, put on your protective gear, spread out your sheet/tarp under it, and put your box on top of it. Firstly, try putting as much of the swarm into the box as possible (using gloved hands or a bee brush). If your swarm is up on a tree, gently shake the

branch to get the bees to fall into the box. If your bees don't stay in the box, it's likely that the queen didn't go into the box with them. If this happens, wait a few minutes for the bees to gather around the queen in a cluster once more and try again. If the cluster is on a small branch, use your pruning shears to remove the branch from the tree/bush and put it into the box with the swarm. Just be sure to remove all the branches/vegetation before you install the swarm into the hive. If the swarm is on a wall or something trickier to navigate, try misting them lightly with water and brushing them into the box. The water makes it more difficult for them to fly away. If your cluster is on the ground, you simply need to pour some lemongrass oil into the box and position the box on its side so it can crawl into it. The lemongrass oil attracts bees.

Installing a Swarm into a New Hive

Once you've got most of the bees in the box, close it and leave a small opening for any remaining bees or scout bees to enter. Be sure to leave the box there until the sun sets to ensure scout bees have enough time to return from their rounds. At nighttime, close the box completely using tape and wrap the swarm in the bed sheet/tarp. Make sure there are air

holes. Be sure to be very careful when transporting the swarm box and installing them into their new hive the following morning. Once you are ready, open the box and shake the bees into the hive. Put the bars and lid back on, and you're done!

To encourage swarming, you can actually set up swarm traps. These work best when they are put in a high place, like up in a tree. Putting a few drops of lemongrass oil in these traps will encourage swarms to enter them.

Bait & Trap

Baiting and trapping is a method that is an extension of swarming, so be sure to read the above info on swarming before reading this part. As you know from before, when swarms form on their "temporary" new base, the scout bees will leave the swarm in search of a new appropriate hive location. Once they find one, they come back to the hive and direct the bees to the new place using a special dance (affectionately called the waggle dance). A few worker bees go to the new location and release a pheromone to make it easier for the other bees to follow them, a pheromone that smells exactly like, you guessed it, lemongrass oil. As mentioned before, lemongrass oil is a great lure to draw bees to a location. So to draw bees into a swarm trap, put a little drop of the oil (you don't need to use too much!) inside and let the oil work its magic.

Splitting

Hive splitting is where a beekeeper **"splits" a pre-existing hive into two by simply removing the hive's frames (or top bars) and moving them into a new hive.** On these frames/top bars, there should be unhatched eggs, nurse bees, and honey from the previous colony. If the bar/frames you remove *don't*

have a queen bee- you don't need to worry too much as the worker bees can raise a new one by feeding an unhatched egg royal jelly. This process cannot happen if the egg has already hatched, so making sure your frames/bars include unhatched eggs is **important.** You can, of course, just buy a queen bee and add them separately, but most beekeepers tend to support the practice of queens being naturally added to a hive instead. The practices used to inseminate queen bees can be problematic, so be sure to do your research before buying a queen bee to see if they have been ethically raised.

To add a "split" to your new hive, you just have to remove a frame/bar from one hive and install it into a new one. It's very, very simple.

Splitting is another popular choice for populating new hives these days as **it's a pretty easy and natural solution and makes the most of a bee colony you already have!** It's also completely free, as you don't need anything more than an existing colony. If you're new to beekeeping, why not try to make some beekeeper friends and strike a deal with them to split one of their existing hives?

CHAPTER 5

Building Your Beehive

"The keeping of bees is like the direction
of sunbeams": Henry David Thoreau

Types of Beehives

There are many different beehive types to choose from, and the type each
beekeeper opts for might vary depending on their location, local climate, or
preferred maintenance style.

The three popular choices are *the Langstroth, the Top-Bar, and the Warre,* so we'll discuss each one here, alongside some of their advantages.

As with many things, *there is no perfect solution,* each hive design has pros and cons. Carefully consider these before choosing the best one for you. The most important point to remember is that there is **no right or wrong way.**

Firstly, let's look at the Langstroth hive.

The Langstroth Hive

The Langstroth hive is the **typical beehive image** that most people think of when you mention beekeeping- the box that has stacked layers. This beehive was created by Rev. LL Langstroth in 1852.

The general idea behind Langstroth is that it's **easy to use, easy to expand, and easy to access.** The breakthrough innovation of this hive design was the inclusion of frames that are **vertically hanging.**

This design also ensured that the gaps between the frames would be at least ¼", thus **accommodating sufficiently for bee space.**

Expanding a Langstroth hive is as simple as adding another layer.

Another huge advantage of the Langstroth hive is that the dimensions of this hive are **pretty universally standard**- so if you buy parts of the hive from various vendors, you shouldn't have too many issues with inconsistent sizing.

The Warre Hive

The Warre hive is *pretty similar to the Langstroth in terms of its shape and design.* This one was created by a French monk called Abbé Émile Warré, whose vision for this hive **mirrors the bee's natural environment.** Due to this, the inside of a Warre hive is *similar to a hollow tree,* where many wild bees choose to build their hive.

The key difference between a Langstroth and Warre hive is that **when adding new boxes to a Warre hive, you add them below the existing boxes.** With the Langstroth, they go on top. Also, the Warre boxes are also *typically a little smaller and lighter.*

Another difference is **the Warre hive often doesn't use foundations**, so bees naturally create comb branching vertically.

The Warre hive's roof (quilt box) is also good at absorbing condensation, which bees really hate.

Overall, it **requires less maintenance,** which might appeal to new beekeepers.

The Top-Bar Hive

The design of the top bar is completely different from the others.

Instead of a stacked, layered design, it's a simple "bathtub"-like shape with frames that run along it.

We'll cover the top bar in much more detail later in this book, so we'll keep it simple.

The advantages of the top-bar hive are that **the frames are much easier to access, and the overall structure is simpler.** You'll see in the next section how many different parts a typical hive requires- but *the top-bar hive doesn't need a lot of them.* It's **easy to use, highly simplistic,** and, similarly to the Warre hive, **mirrors bees' natural environment as it lacks foundations.**

The Elements of a Beehive

The Basic Set-Up

As we previously discussed, the beehive is not as simple as a wooden box with a few frames inside- it's an incredibly complex structure with many components designed to *keep the bees happy and maximize their honey production as much as possible*! Most modern designs are also designed for safety and ease of use. A beehive where you can easily and safely harvest your honey is much more preferable than one that makes the job difficult and stressful.

As a beginner beekeeper looking at a hive can be pretty overwhelming, so let's get into all the different components a typical beehive contains and break them down.

As discussed in the previous section, several different beehives are still commonly used in beekeeping. But the good news for you is that **they all function similarly, so they** mostly have the same setup internally.

The Hive Set-Up

The layers of a typical beehive are as follows (the point at the top of the list represents the actual top of the beehive and going down as an actual beehive would):

Top of the hive

- Outer Cover

- Feeders (internal hive top feeders)

- Inner Cover

- Honey Super/Extracting Super

- Queen Excluder

- Frames

- Brood Box

- Slatted Rack

- Entrance Reducer

- Bottom Board

- Hive Stand

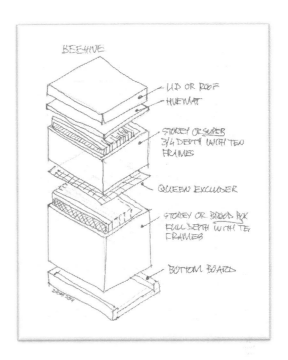

Ground

Let's look at the beehive structure in more detail and break down each layer one by one. **This structure is based on the widely popular Langstroth hive,** but many hives (including the Top-Bar hive we'll teach you how to build later) are structured similarly.

Outer Cover

The outer cover, sometimes called the "telescoping cover," is there to act as the roof of the hive. Protecting your hive and the bees inside is essential from bad weather conditions. Generally, outer covers are flat and are topped with a type of metal sheet (such as aluminum, zinc, steel, or copper) to offer more safety from rain. The material of the outer cover is important, but what's more important is ensuring that the cover's dimensions are wider than that of the actual hive to ensure the entire hive is protected. The outer cover should also fit down over the edge of the inner cover to offer further protection.

Feeders

As we mentioned before, feeders are pretty important because they offer your worker bees nourishment when there isn't enough spare honey to go around. Even bees, as clever and efficient as they are, need a little help sometimes. When it comes to feeders, there are

many types; some are attached to the hive entrance, some are put between the frames inside the hive, and some are even just left outside rather haphazardly. The type you choose is really a matter of personal preference.

One *big advantage of having internally-located feeders is the fact that they're less attractive to robbing bees* or other predators of that kind.

Also, it's much more comfortable for your bees to have a food source **they can find inside their hive.**

If you're putting your feeder internally, you need it to sit directly above the brood box, allowing the bees to get to it easily. But if you do this, don't forget to remove the queen excluder layer, as this will make it harder for the bees to reach it!

One common type of feeder is an **internal hive top feeder.** These are good because they *can hold a lot of sugar syrup* and even include special trinkets that prevent the bees from falling into the syrup and drowning. This type of feeder is *most appropriate when you need to feed a large colony of bees from one source.*

Another option for a feeder is similar to the last one, but the external version: is an **external hive top feeder.** These feeders are typically made from mason jars or plastic buckets filled with sugar syrup. These *vessels are turned upside down over the inner cover's entrance hole and are typically surrounded by a simple empty hive box.* This option is good for *protecting the syrup from robbing bees, as well as certain bad weather conditions.*

One more example of a commonly used feeder is a feeding shim. A feeding shim is another empty wooden box with the same dimensions as a hive, filled with feeding vessels. These are *a popular choice for providing bees with sugar candy during the coldest months of the year.*

Inner Cover

The inner cover is essentially the ceiling of the hive. It includes an entrance hole in the center and another entrance notch at the front of the cover. When installing the cover, **this entrance must be facing forwards.** The holes mentioned above are really important, as *they ensure that the hive can stay well-ventilated.* These holes can also be used to insert feeders into the hive or act as an escape hole for the bees while you're harvesting honey.

The **best type of inner cover is one made from plywood**, as ones made from other materials will sag with age- bad when you're trying to conserve space inside your hive.

It's **really easy for people to install their inner covers incorrectly, so be sure to take care when doing this!** Inner covers have what is referred to as a "summer" and "winter" position; for most of the year, your covers should remain in the "summer" position. One side of the cover is flat, and another side has a frame around the edge that has a shallow open space. To **position the cover in a summer position, the flat side should be facing down, and the framed side should be facing up.** This position allows an air gap between the inner and outer covers, which keeps the hive a little cooler.

Honey Supers

The honey super is the layer that is positioned above the queen excluder and brood boxes. This layer is the one that is dedicated to housing the honey that your bees will tirelessly produce. Super boxes usually come in two sizes, medium and shallow, and they're *typically smaller than the brood box itself.* If you opt for a smaller-sized honey super, your **bees will**  **probably fill the supers with honey more evenly,** but the medium-sized supers are the most common.

When it comes time to harvest honey from your hives, **you'll do so by collecting it from the supers.** Just don't forget to leave enough honey for your bees to survive through the winter.

Queen Excluder

The queen excluder is a layer that *helps to split the hive into two very important parts; the part where honey is stored and the part when eggs are laid.* The two should not be mixed for obvious reasons. The queen excluder sits on the top of the brood box and is a kind of mesh that is too tight for the queen to go through (hence the name). It prevents the queen from accessing the honey supers, so **she can't lay eggs there.**

There are queen excluders available made from all kinds of materials- metal, plastic, wood, etc.

The use of queen excluders is actually *a bit controversial* among beekeepers. Some see this layer as **an essential protocol for ensuring an organized and efficient hive, but others see it as unnecessary as it apparently causes stress for the worker bees** (who don't like squeezing through small holes and don't like to move anywhere without the queen). However, **if you're a beginner, we'd strongly recommend using one** as the techniques you'll need to use to avoid needing a queen excluder are a little more tricky.

Frames

Every single type of beehive uses some type of frame. **A beehive without frames is simply not a beehive.** A beehive's frame shape will depend on the type of hive, but it'll always be there in some form.

The frame is the base on which the bees will construct their honeycomb. For beekeepers, the act of making honeycomb is referred to as "drawing comb."

Frames often have a " foundation " sheet on them; basically, a *hexagonal pattern made out of pressed wax or plastic*. This pattern **acts as a template the bees can use to build their honeycomb onto**- it helps the comb *come out neater and more concise*. But of course, a foundation sheet is not an essential thing to use; **some beekeepers prefer not to use them at all**. Frames without foundation are appropriately named "foundationless frames."

The frames themselves are **typically made from wood**, but it's not unheard of for beekeepers to use plastic. Of course, the size of the frame you use needs to match the size of your hive. Frames will come available in three sizes; **shallow, medium,** and **deep**. The "deep" frames are usually found in brood boxes, as they need to be a little bigger. Whereas shallow and medium frames are most commonly used for honey supers of a corresponding size.

Most frames you can buy on the market come in similar sizes, but every brand won't be perfectly the same- so make sure to check the frames can fit into the hive you have/want before purchasing them.

To avoid issues with compromising bee space (*see next section for more on bee space),* it's a **good idea to use frames that are the same type/size within one hive.**

Brood Box

The brood box is the lowest box in the hive and contains the "brood,"; A.K.A., the area where the queen lays her eggs. It's also where the queen lives. **The brood box should be the largest part of the hive as it needs to accommodate the growth of the bee colony** throughout the appropriate season. If the brood box doesn't have sufficient space, a second brood box can be added to provide some extra room.

A brood box is made up of several frames that bees use to make wax comb. How many frames the brood box has depends on the type of hive you have (but it will probably be around 8 or 10). If you don't mind the extra weight, 10 frames are okay, but if you need to be able to transport your hive for some reason, be sure to consider this, as a 10-frame brood box can get heavy very quickly. **If you want a lighter hive- fewer frames are better**. But *if* *your priority is to produce as much honey as possible and expand your colony, then a 10-frame box might be better.*

Extra: brood boxes are referred to by many names, including "brood chamber," "deep hive body," and even "deep supers" or "brood supers." But using "super" within the name can confuse new beekeepers- make sure that the brood box and the honey supers are not confused, as these are two very important and separate parts. The super honey layer should **sit above the brood boxes,** separated by a queen excluder. Don't get them mixed up!

Slatted Rack (optional)

As you can see in the title, this is an optional part of the hive, but many beekeepers swear by using them, so it depends on your preference. A slatted rack, also called a brood rack, is **part of a hive that helps prevent issues such as congestion or ventilation.** When your hive is at its most populated, it can get a little crowded during the height of the season! Using a slatted rack provides the bees with a little extra space to move around below the brood box. It's **great for preventing overcrowding and keeping your hive well-ventilated.**

Adding additional space using a slatted rack *also helps keep your hive warmer during winter.*

If you want to use a slatted rack, just *be sure that you're putting it in the right way.* A slatted rack will have a deep and shallow side; the shallow side should be positioned upwards and in line with your brood box frames. If you don't put it in this way, the bees are likely to fill the extra space with burr comb, making it a little harder for you to maintain and remove your brood box frames.

Entrance Reducer

The role of the entrance reducer is **literally to reduce the size of the entrance to the hive.** This part is located snugly between the bottom board and the lowest hive box, and they're *very useful for controlling movement into the hive.* They can also be used to prevent other pests from entering your hive (e.g., stopping field mice from entering the hive in the winter months). In the event that your hive gets "robbed" by predators, **having a limited entrance space helps bees be able to defend the hive more easily**.

The entrance reducer is a long piece of wood with several different-sized holes acting as entrances. The wood is adjusted by turning it to change the entrance size to the hive.

The main piece of advice we can give when shopping for this piece of gear is to buy an entrance reducer from the same manufacturer that makes your other hive parts. This is to avoid frustration, as different brands are not the most consistent when it comes to sizing.

Bottom Board

The bottom board is essentially the floor of the hive. There are two types: solid or screened.

Screened: a screened bottom board is **great for ventilation** as it is a mesh screen typically made from wire or plastic. It helps to r**egulate an appropriate temperature within the hive** and can also **help limit humidity**. This screen board is also thought to be *better at protecting the hive from pests such as moths or varroa* (a type of mite that can cause a lot of problems in beehives). As the screen has holes in it, it allows things to fall through it, which **can also help to keep the hive a little cleaner**.

A decent-quality screened bottom board will come with some kind of tray that can be slid shut to close the bottom of the hive. This is useful during the colder months and when you want to inspect the hive.

Solid: as you might guess, a solid bottom board is **a board that has no holes**. Using this type, *ventilation can be reduced greatly*, and in colder weather, it has the advantage of keeping the bottom of the hive much warmer. The warmer hive will encourage bees to start getting to work (or *brood rearing*) earlier in the day. As solid bottom boards don't have holes for waste and other things to fall through, this type of board will catch a lot of various debris. Due to this, a *solid bottom board needs to be cleaned regularly.*

Hive Stand

The hive stand is the structure where the whole hive will be put on top, and it's a crucial part of the hive set-up for countless reasons. Firstly, it *stops unwanted moisture from entering the hive.* When it comes to wild beehives, they're typically located in trees or as high up as possible- because bees hate moisture and want to avoid humidity

as much as possible. In fact, **if too much damp enters a hive, it can kill a bee colony.**

Another key reason to use a hive stand is that *it'll be easier for you to maintain your hive.* Having to bend over to do all necessary bee-related tasks can mess with your back, so having an elevated hive base will make life far easier.

The **perfect height for a hive stand is typically considered to be 2 feet/60 cm.**

When looking at what type of hive stand to buy, there are two types available; single and multiple. Single hive stands are often bought commercially, whereas beekeepers themselves often build multiple hive stand*s*. The main benefit of having a multiple hive stand is **that there will be sufficient room between hives for inspecting them,** as inspection requires you to take apart your hive, and you'll need room to put these parts down. These hive stand types *can be made from wooden beams or cement blocks.*

If you're looking to build a multiple hive stand, just remember that the stand needs to support a lot of weight and **be as level to the ground as possible.**

You can also build single hive stands, but it's far easier to just buy one that you can simply assemble. Even if you're dealing with an uneven surface, a single hive stand can be stabilized easily; they're far more forgiving. Just make sure you're getting a hive stand that fits your hive size (depending on whether it's an 8 or 10-frame hive).

Depending on the type of hive stand you purchase, some will come with an additional *landing board,* which is a kind of ramp that bees going in and out of the hive can utilize. Most agree that a landing board is good additional equipment for new beekeepers, as **it gives them a chance to observe the colony before they disappear inside the hive**. Even a *few minutes of simple observation is enough to learn a lot about bees' habits and behaviors*!

But landing boards are not necessary for the bee's daily life, so **they are not essential pieces of kit to have.** In fact, experts say that these boards can hinder honeybees from living in certain climate*s.* Also, in certain weather conditions, these ramps can pose a bit of a problem: if it snows, the entrance can get blocked, or if it rains, *the bees can get stuck* to it.

Considering Bee Space

While modern beehives are designed for ease of use and safety, they are also designed to cater to how bees like to move around the hive to ensure **their comfort and security**; A.K.A.

bee space! We have already mentioned bee space in the above section, but here we'll cover **why it's so important** and more info about what it is exactly.

Bee space refers to **the amount of free space available for bees within the hive to move around** and get things done. It's an area of typically around 1cm that the bees will not fill with honeycomb so they can easily circulate.

Bee space may seem unimportant, but it is *essential to ensuring that bees can operate well.* It's important we consider this space when constructing a beehive as it serves a very useful secondary function- it gives us a small area to open the hive without damaging any honeycomb!

The first hive design to pay attention to "bee space" was the Langstroth hive (see the picture). To this day, the Langstroth hive is one of the most popular design choices for beekeepers.

Another reason bee space is so important is that ignoring it and leaving too much free space in the hive **will lead to bees constructing burr comb to fill the void.** This can be an issue as the burr comb is constructed randomly, so it can easily get messy and makes removing parts of the hive much *more difficult.* To deal with unwanted burr comb, the hives should be checked for it regularly, and they should be removed (CAREFULLY) if found.

You should be especially careful when inspecting your hive for burr comb, as **the queen will often use burr comb as a place to lay eggs**- so when removing the burr comb, you could accidentally remove the queen from the hive. Be sure to check everything carefully and thoroughly before removing it from the hive or disposing of it.

CHAPTER 6

The Best Location for Your Beehive

When deciding where the best place to put your apiary is, there are many points to think about! You can't just throw it anywhere and hope for the best. The best location for you and your bees will **take into consideration your bee colony's needs, your convenience, and the type of honey you want to produce.** The difference between a good and a bad location could be significant.

In this section, we'll cover the following location-related factors in detail:

1. Southeast Facing Entrance

2. Wind

3. Sunlight

4. Food

5. Water

6. Dry Ground

7. Flat Land

8. Low Foot Traffic

9. Space Between Beehives

Firstly, where is a bee's natural habitat?

When raising a bee colony, it's important to consider the bee's natural habitat as **we want to try and assimilate that as far as we can.** Naturally, bees build hives up in trees, ideally somewhere between a wooded area and a flower field- giving them security, keeping them dry and shaded, and allowing easy access to pollen.

When putting bees into a hive (e.g., taking them from natural habitat to a man-made one), these are the factors we need to focus on to keep our bees happy and productive.

Southeast Facing Entrance (according to your location)

Bees won't care too much if their hive entrance isn't facing southeast, but **doing so has multiple benefits**.

The first reason is because of *sunlight*, the morning sun rises from the south or southeast (depending on where you're located). *Facing your hive towards the sunrise will help your bees be more productive in the morning*, as bees won't start working until the hive heats up. The morning sun can provide a nice bit of warmth for them to kick start their day.

The second reason is that *the strongest winds typically come from the northwest* (again, depending on where you're located). Facing the entrance away from that wind **prevents your bees from dealing with colder temperatures and excessive ventilation**. It'll also be far easier for your bees to exit the hive when they do not have to fight against gales.

Suppose you're unsure which direction best positions your beehive entrance in your local environment. In that case, it's a *good idea to contact your local bee association* to ask what beekeepers in your area tend to do- or if you have any beekeeper friends, then just ask them!

Wind

Naturally, bees choose spaces for their hives that are **robust and shielded from wind** (inside tree trunks, for example), as they *don't want their hive to be damaged or blown away*. The last thing you want is for your hive to be blown over, **especially if you have several bee boxes stacked together.**

So, make sure to either choose a location that will be *sufficiently protected from excessive wind* or consider putting up a wind barrier to protect your hive. Once you've figured out what direction the wind is likely to come from in your location, consider putting your hive behind a structure, a wall, a wide tree, etc. If you don't have any of the above, you can make a makeshift structure using a fence or tarp, etc.

Considering wind is especially important in the winter, as the chill from winter winds can be very destructive. To limit your hive's exposure to the wind during the winter, **make sure to use a solid bottom board in your hive** (see the previous section for info about this).

Sunlight

It can be a little tricky for beekeepers to figure out how much sun their hive needs. Most assume that the more sunlight, the better. But **bees typically prefer a hive location that is cooler and more shaded.** For bees, *safety and comfort are their top priorities*, so even though bees are more productive in sunlight, they don't consider that too much when picking the perfect spot for their hive.

There are downsides, however, to putting hives in the shade. They're *more likely to experience issues such as mold, hive beetle infestation, various diseases, and other pests.* A lot of these issues can be fixed/prevented by direct sunlight exposure. So actually, **most experts recommend putting your hive in an area that gets direct sunlight** due to this. It really does depend on your local climate, though. If you live in a place where the temperature gets pretty high (such as the south and southwest of the US), it's *probably better to give your hive a little shade.* You **want to prevent your bees from overheating as much as possible.**

Seeing your bees exhibit certain behaviors, such as bearding (see the picture) or fanning, means the hive is too hot. This disturbs their productivity and can damage both the bees and the hive itself.

Food

When it comes to food, **the closer, the better.** Bees will travel up to 6 miles for food, but only if they're desperate.

This point is pretty self-explanatory, but there are a few extra things to mention:

- If there is a farm nearby that you want your bees to pollinate, be sure to **check that the farmer doesn't use pesticides.** Pesticides can cause a lot of problems for bees, so they are best avoided when possible.

- If you have a garden where you want your bees to pollinate, **you don't need to put your beehives right next to it.** As we'll mention in this section, you *should avoid places with high foot traffic*, so if people are commonly traipsing through your garden, then it's not a good place for happy bees.

Water

Bees need water like most creatures! If the weather is hot, *a beehive can drink a whole gallon of water.* It's a common misconception that bees exclusively consume honey; actually, *they only really eat honey during the winter for extra energy.* Bees are great at finding water sources, but make sure to put your hives nearby **to make their lives a little easier and optimize their working time.** If you have the option to, installing a pond near your beehives would be a great water source for them. Just remember that *bees can't swim, so putting your hive next to a deep water source could be risky!* It's better to **provide a drinking source that is either shallow or contains rocks or pebbles that they can stand on** while drinking.

Dry Ground

As we've discussed in previous sections, the main thing bees hate is moisture. So **putting your hive in a**

dry place is pretty important. This is especially important to consider if you live in a climate where it rains regularly, as *rainfall can cause the earth to sink and will make your hive uneven* (which will disrupt your bee's comb production and make their comb uneven or messy).

Also, in general, it's **a good idea to avoid "marshy" ground** when placing your beehive, as beehives can get pretty heavy! A *typical hive can easily weigh above 100 pounds.*

If your area is subject to rain often and you don't have any "dry ground" patches to choose from, then *make your own.* You could put down a small patch of decking, some stones, or pavement to place your hive on.

Flat Land

We touched on this a little in the last point, but here we're focusing on land with natural elevation (e.g., hills and valleys).

The biggest problem with putting your hive in a valley is that *naturally, a lot of cold air will travel through it.*

Another problem with placing hives in areas like valleys or hills is that **it makes them very tricky to move them if you need to.** A medium-sized hive can weigh a hefty 60 pounds when filled with honey- a lot of weight to carry up and down a hill.

Low Foot Traffic

As we mentioned before, it's preferable to put your hive in an area that doesn't have a lot of people wandering around. Bees generally **prefer to be in hives in isolated areas,** so it's not a good idea to put your apiary close to an area where children play, or cars regularly pass, etc.

For this reason, it's also often *not recommended for beekeepers to put their hives too close to their living quarters, their garden, a playground, a shared property line, etc.*

If you're unsure what to do about the available space, just make sure that your hives are **at least 20 feet away from any area where people/animals often go or make noise**. As we mentioned before, having something like a tree or fence near your hive is a

good idea to shield it from the wind. If you do this, *ensure the entrance is not facing toward the object* to avoid difficulty for the bees getting in or out.

In the "food" section, we mentioned not putting your bees too close to your garden, and this is because *it'll just make gardening a lot harder if you have a load of bees constantly zooming around.* Bees **typically fly at a speed of 15 mph,** which will make it a little painful if they run into you. Your bees will find your garden; you don't need to put them in it or next to it for them to locate it.

Extra: It's important to note the types of flowers your bees visit when they produce honey so that you can keep track of the "type" of honey being produced. Some flower's pollen will actually add toxic qualities to the honey produced from it, such as rhododendron ponticum (a special rhododendron that grows in Turkey)- honey made with pollen from this flower contains the grayanotoxin, which can cause dizziness, nausea, and convulsions if consumed. **Be sure to do your research!**

Space Between Beehives

It's a general rule of thumb and somewhat common sense that **you shouldn't be putting your hives right next to each other.** You probably knew that...but did you know that **there should be at least 6 feet between them?** This is partially for your bee's comfort but *mainly because it gives you sufficient space to work on your hive and maneuver your hive tool.* If you're a little limited in space, consider using 8-frame hives (instead of 10) and make sure they have **at least 3 feet between them.**

One potential issue that can occur from putting your hives right next to each other is that *bees might abandon the hive* (abscond) or *rob each other* (steal another hive's stored honey). New beekeepers share this common fear, and placing the hives further away may seem like a logical way to fix this. But actually, *your bees are going to try to rob each other no matter what you do.* One way to **reduce this is by using an entrance reducer on your hive** and setting it to the smallest opening.

Extra- How to Stop Bees Absconding

There are a few reasons why bees might abandon their hive: *lack of food/resources, they have not sufficiently adapted to it, there are frequent disturbances from pests/humans/dampness*, etc.

The best way to prevent bees from absconding is to **put another queen excluder between the bottom board and the brood chamber.** This *prevents absconding as it makes it harder for them to leave,* so they're more likely to adapt to their environment. Also, this queen excluder will *make it impossible for the queen to leave,* and **many bees will be reluctant to leave without their queen**. See the previous section for more info on queen excluders.

Be sure to come back to these points when considering where to place your new apiary.

Now, let's look at how to put an actual hive together!

CHAPTER 7

How to Build a "Top Bar Hive" Step-by-Step

"Every human being should show the greatest interest in beekeeping because our lives depend on it": Rudolf Steiner

Before we get into the step-by-step guide on actually putting your hive together, let's look at some general advice for building your hive.

General Hive Structure Advice

- It's a good idea for beginners to use a hive with **two brood boxes and three medium-sized supers,** but the simplistic design of a top-bar hive means you won't need to worry about this, as this design doesn't use these elements.

- If you're putting your hive together yourself from parts you've purchased, it's **better not to order parts from various places** as the **dimensions may not be consistent,** and you could end up with a hive that won't fit together.

- If you're making your hive from scratch, the most commonly used material is **pine wood which has been painted.**

  - Pinewood will deteriorate over time due to the elements, so *coating the surface with a 20:1 mix of linseed oil and beeswax* or simply *painting it* will *help to extend its life.*

  - If you can source some **red cedar wood,** this is a great choice for building a hive, as it lasts far longer and doesn't need any paint due to protection from the wood's natural oils. But it's pricey, so treated pine wood is more common.

What is a Top-Bar Hive?

The top-bar hive is **one of the oldest hive designs in domestic beekeeping-** with the first reported usage being from the 1600s.

People build top-bar hives from all kinds of materials- but the most commonly used one is **some form of protected/painted wood.**

A top-bar hive is a **long rectangular shape**, somewhat similar to a bathtub or trough. The hive contains *several frames hanging down from the top, where the bees build a comb that runs from the top* to the bottom. These frames *don't typically need a foundation, as gravity does most of the work in guiding the bees* to construct the comb. Due to this, most people say that the top-bar hive *encourages a more natural and authentic bee environment.* Top-bar enthusiasts are beekeepers who typically prefer to observe their bees in a condition as close to the real thing as possible.

Top-Bar Hive Benefits

- Because of the horizontal design, **you won't need to lift heavy boxes or agitate your bees** as much when harvesting honey.
- The design means the hive's structure is **far more minimal** than the traditional "stacked" beehive style that we discussed earlier: with a top-bar hive; you *don't need honey supers, foundation, extra frames, uncapping knives, extractors, queen excluders, etc.* This makes it **a fantastic choice for beginners!**
- The **combs are much easier to remove**, making life simpler and means your bees will be more forgiving when you do. So it's *generally easier for a beginner to handle.*
- Most top-hive bars have a long "window" that runs along the side, which lets you **observe your bees hard at work without disturbing them.**

Top-Bar Hive Maintenance

As we've mentioned a few times, the maintenance of a top-bar hive is far easier than other designs as it's a much more minimal design.

Bee Space

For basic management, the main thing you have to check is **whether your bees have enough space**. As your colony grows, you'll need to move the divider boards down your hive and add more bars to accommodate them. After you harvest the honey, **you need to lessen the empty space in your hive,** so the bees have less space to heat up during the colder months.

Luckily, the *side window in the top-bar hive makes checking bee space super easy and fast.*

Comb

Considering comb, bees in top-bar hives **usually attach their comb to the inner hive walls.** So you'll probably have to pull this comb off the walls before you take any frames out, but this *can easily be done with a hive tool.*

Honey

Harvesting honey from a top-bar hive is really easy also. You must **cut the comb from the top bars, then crush and strain the honey out.** Simple.

Now we've covered all the essential extra info- let's learn how to actually put one together!

Building a Top-Bar Hive: Step-by-Step

This project will take **roughly 8 hours to complete** and makes a **36" long hive.** The tutorial here is building a top-bar hive *upside down and inside out,* so consider that when putting it together.

This tutorial uses **well-seasoned pine** (pine coated in a 20:1 concoction of linseed oil and beeswax; *instructions for this coating can be found at the end of the tutorial*).

Make sure to read through all the instructions first before starting.

For this project, you'll need:

- A **quantity of timber** that is around **1" thick and 12" wide** (or 25mm x 300mm). If you can't find boards that are 12" wide, just glue two 6" boards together. If you can't find 1" thick wood, 3/4" will be okay, but thicker wood will be *better insulated and longer lasting.*

- To make a **36" hive,** you need **three wood pieces of 12" by 36",** with **one of them cut into two pieces of 18" by 12"** to make the ends.

- The floorboard of the hive will be either a **36" by 6" piece** or some simple mesh of the same size. The **legs will be the same size** but **cut lengthwise to be 3" wide.**

    o For the mesh floor (for all times of the year except the cold winter months), you'll need a **piece of plastic or stainless mesh with around 8-10 holes to each inch** and a **handful of pins (flat-headed)** to fix it to the frame.

- You'll also require a **board of 11" by at least 25" for the follower boards** and 30 ft of 1 1/4" by 3/4" straight timber for the top bars.

- For the hive body, you'll also need **twelve 2.5" (60mm) stainless steel or brass wood screws** and **eight 2" (50mm) galvanized or stainless bolts** with nuts and washers.

- For tools, you need **a plane, a carpenter's saw, a screwdriver, a drill, a square, and clamps**. A **bench-mounted circular saw,** or **power drill** would be useful if available.

- You'll need a strong external grade glue that is waterproof for all permanent joints. You can use **epoxy resin glue** if you wish, but it's not necessary.

Let's get into it!

To Make the Top Bars

- The top bar hive's most critical part is deciding the top bar's width. Most people recommend a width from 1 1/4" to 1 3/8" (32-35mm). If you ask local experts and they recommend something different, follow that. It **can be a matter of trial and error**- if you build this hive and find your bees require more space, adjust the next set of bars you make accordingly.

- To make the top bars, you'll need to **cut a saw kerf down the center of the bottom of the bar using a circular saw**- it doesn't need to go all the way to the ends, but it'll be easier to cut it like that. The **groove needs to be at least 1/8" deep and the width of your saw blade**. Once you've made this groove, **fill it with boiled beeswax and leave it to cool**. This will provide your bees with a base to build their beeswax on when the frames are in place.

Assembling the Hive

- First, you need to put together your materials and cut and glue all the boards to the necessary sizes listed above. Make the sides and ends first, and while the glue is setting, make the important follower boards.

  - To do this: **glue & screw or pin a 17" top bar along the top edge of each of your follower boards.** If you place thin strips of wood underneath while doing this, it helps to ensure the wood is laterally centered. **Clamp the wood pieces together** while they set.

- To make the follower boards, you need **an 11" or 12" board that is 1/2" thick.** Mark the board **15" across at the top and halfway along at 7.5".**

- At each mark, **draw a line from top to bottom and mark 2.5" on either side of the point** at the bottom edge.

- Join up the **bottom dots with the top dots** (not the middle line) to *form a trapezoidal shape.* Extend your shape to make an identical upside shape on the other side of it- **this helps to save wood.**

- **Glue and pin/screw a top bar along the top edge of each follower board** (centered). Clamp them and *leave them to dry overnight.*

Making the Legs

- You'll need **4 legs which are 3" by 2"** (75 by 50 mm) and **at a height that you prefer (typically around 30")**. *If you're in a wheelchair, a height of 26" may be more appropriate.*

  - You don't need to use legs if you don't want to, as this hive would work just as well sitting on some stand or base; **just make sure it's stable!** It's just *important that your hive is not sitting directly on the ground,* as this will make your hive a treasure trove for all kinds of pests.

- If using legs, they **need to be bolted to your hive's end pieces with stainless steel or galvanized nuts and 2" bolts.** Put the washers under the heads of the bolts and nuts, as this will prevent them from damaging the wood.

  - **DO NOT USE WOOD SCREWS.** They're a lot cheaper, yes, but they're *unreliable* and pretty much guarantee disaster will ensue.

- Firstly, get your follower boards and *invert them.* Place them on your bench parallel to each other, **between 18" and 24" apart.**

- Position one of your side panels lying flat against the follower boards, resting on the top bars to form the side of the hive.

- Put the other side panel on the other side.

- Once both your side panels are in place, put an end piece on one end, with its bottom edge lying flat on the bench. This *gives clearance space for the top bars.*

- With the end piece in position, use a pencil to **draw a line where the edges of the side panel touch the end piece** (inside and outside of the side panel).

- Take away the end pieces, and inside the shape you marked (where the side panels will eventually sit), **mark three points where you will drill holes for screws.** It doesn't matter if the screws are perfectly distanced; *just try and eyeball it,* so they're equally spaced apart (and **not too close to the ends**).

- For drilling, **use a drill bit slightly larger than the screw shank.** The screws you should be using for this part should be **stainless steel or brass ones that are a minimum of 2.5" long.**

- Put your two end pieces on top of each other **to save time,** with the one with your guides on top, and drill holes where you marked earlier. After you drill the first few holes, *put some screws in them (lightly) to help make sure the boards don't move while you're screwing them.*

- If you're using legs, use your drilling time to put some bolt holes into your legs. You want to **mark a point that is 5" from the top of your leg (in the center) and draw a line straight down to the bottom of your leg.** This line is where the outer edge of your leg will lie. Drill a **hole minimum 3" from the leg's top edge, and a lower hole 10" from the top.** The top of your leg will be trimmed to accommodate the lid. Make sure that the lower hole sits comfortably outside of the sidewall line. The holes you drill in the legs should allow the legs to match up with the holes in your end pieces, so use that as a guide if you're not sure.

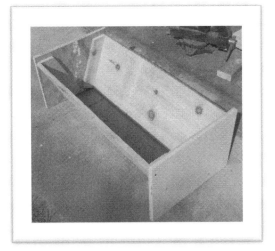

- As we said, the roof frame will sit on the legs. Line your legs up to your end pieces and mark a straight line along where the top edge of your end piece is; **it should be around 2" from the top of your leg**. Use a saw to make an indentation, but **don't cut all the way through.**

For the Floor (mesh)

- When the weather is colder, *it's better to use a solid floor* (as we've previously discussed), but **mesh flooring is a far better choice for most of the year and for easy hive maintenance.**

- We recommend using a **heavy-duty plastic garden mesh** for the job, as it's robust but also flexible.

- Simply lie your mesh on the bottom of the hive cavity and cut the mesh, so it fits the hole as perfectly as possible.

- On the inside, it's a *good idea to cut some rough pieces of wood and use them as a kind of doorstop against the mesh* to ensure it's sealed tightly and nothing can sneak in. Make sure you cut these pieces, so they fit snugly against the shape of your follower boards.

- If you want to use a solid floor, you can put **a 6" by 3/4" piece of timber under your hive**, attached using some brass snap-locks or hinges etc.

Entrance

- Now you've got a box of some form; your bees need a way to enter! For this, **drill a few holes (at least 3 are recommended) that are at least 1" in diameter and 2" from the base of your**

hive. It's a good idea to put the entrances close together in the center of the side of your hive, but make sure to **put at least 3" between each hole.**

- You can add a few more entrances on the other side or another **at least 4 or 5" from the end of the hive.**

Roof frame

- Before attaching the frame, finally, **attach your legs using the previously mentioned screws.**
- The roof frame consists of a simplistic *rectangle frame made of 3" by 3/4" timber which has been screwed or glued at the corners.* **Don't forget to leave about 1/4" slack both ways** to allow for wood movement- if your roof jams, it'll be quite annoying.

Roof

- For a simple roof, you can use a **sheet of corrugated plastic.** It's not a great option for isolation in colder months, but it's *good as a temporary solution.*

- Use a triangular gable roof for a more elegant-looking choice. This is also better for times that it rains, as *the water will just slide right off.* You can use any material, but anything light is a good choice.

Finishing touches

- The last thing to do is to coat your hive to protect it from the elements.

- If you used red cedar wood, you could skip this step, but otherwise, most beekeepers recommend using something like Cuprinol, Creosote, paint, or varnishes to coat your hive.

- We previously mentioned the *linseed and beeswax solution*, and we'll explain how to make that here.

  - Heat in a **double boiler** (or a bain Marie) **a mixture of 1:20 linseed oil to melt beeswax** (e.g., 1-liter raw linseed oil to 50ml beeswax).

  - Heat until as hot as possible and **stir for 10 minutes.**

  - Leave to cool a little and *paint onto your hive while still rather warm.*

  - When painting, **pay attention to coating the end grain, joints, and underneath nail heads.**

  - You **don't need to coat the hive inside**, as the bees will do that.

And you're done!

CHAPTER 8

How to Harvest Honey

" Life is the flower for which love is the honey.": Victor Hugo

So you've got your hive, you've got your bees, you've set them up in a good location. Now what? **Let's look at how to actually harvest your honey**. In the next chapter, we'll look at beeswax, so skip ahead if that's what you're looking for.

What to Know Beforehand

We're going to walk you through a very simple step-by-step guide on how to harvest your honey. But, firstly- **when should you harvest your honey?**

*The greatest "honey flow" is typically **when the flowers are fully bloomed**- so around **June or July**. Early spring will have a lighter honey flow, but **the timing will vary depending on your geographic location**.*

General Advice from the Experts

- To avoid contamination, you should always use a clean comb/tool when collecting honey.

- If you harvest your honey in the **spring,** then **the honey will be lighter in color and milder in flavor.** Honey harvested **later in the season will be darker, with a more intense flavor.** When you harvest depends on your taste preference or the type of honey you want to sell.

- Check before you harvest that your honey cells are **at least 90% capped** (covered in wax); if not capped enough, **the honey is not ready for extraction.**
  - Honey harvested too early (while not sufficiently "capped") is **referred to as "green" honey**; it's not only **unsafe to eat** but also super gooey and not great tasting.

- You can harvest honey as late as September, but **it'll be tougher to extract if it's colder.**
  - The *ideal temperature to extract honey is between 75 and 80 degrees.*

- **Avoid harvesting honey from the bottom 2 boxes of your hive**- these stores will be used as food by your bees in the winter.
  - You should leave at least **80 pounds of honey** in these boxes for your colony to survive.

Note: if you have protective gear, **do not forget to put it on before you open your hive.** It's better to be safe than sorry!

Now we've covered the basics, let's get to the good part:

How to Harvest

1. Open your Hive

With your trusty smoker in hand and ready to go, **approach your beehive from behind and shoot some smoke around the hive's entrance.** Take off the top and release smoke just above the cavity *to encourage your bees to go to the bottom of the box.* If your inner cover doesn't open due to propolis or burr comb, *use your hive tool to pry it open* (being careful not to damage any comb while doing so).

2. *Remove the Bees from your Frame*

After removing the frame you wish to harvest from, you may notice some straggler bees clinging to it. Most of your bees will stay in the hive because of the smoke, but *some might be a little more stubborn.* Get your bee brush and **very gently push the bees from the frame back into the hive cavity** to make uncapping your honey easier.

3. *Uncap your Honey Cells*

Use an **uncapping device to remove the wax from the honey cells on the frame-** *don't forget to do it on both sides!* If the wax layer is particularly thick, using an uncapping knife will make your life a lot easier.

3. *Extract your Honey using a Honey Extractor*

A honey extractor is a **manual or electric machine that spins the frames to force honey out of the cells** while **protecting the wax.** Process your frames using this machine to extract the honey.

4. *Strain your Honey*

Run your honey **through a filter or some layers of cheesecloth** to get rid of any stray bits of comb or other debris.

5. *Store your Honey*

Depending on the size of your yield, put your honey in food-safe containers. A large IFA food-grade bucket would be good for bigger yields, *but for smaller yields, simple quart glass jars or smaller food-grade buckets.* If you're reusing glass jars, **ensure they've been sterilized first.**

NOTE: It's **not recommended to store your honey in containers made of metal**, as *a chemical reaction can occur.*

And that's it! Collecting honey is probably the easiest, as well as the most gratifying, part of the whole process.

CHAPTER 9

Beeswax 101

"Pleasant words are a honeycomb; sweet to the soul
and healing to the bones.": Proverb 16:24

In this chapter, we'll go over all the basics of beeswax- one of the core ingredients you can harvest from your beehive. We'll cover briefly **how beeswax is produced, how you can harvest it, and what you can do with it.**

Firstly, what exactly is it?

Beeswax is a **natural wax that worker bees use to form "combs"** to house their honey eventually. It is also often *used to repair and recycle existing combs.*

Beeswax is made up of **mainly natural alcohol and fatty acids**. Worker bees make it in a special wax-producing gland found in their abdomen (which basically processes sugar from pollen and turns it into wax) and place it strategically in the hive- the pollen they collect helps to give the beeswax its "golden" coloring.

The fact that beeswax is **such a robust and stable ingredient** (especially in both hot and cold weather conditions) makes it *not only perfect for constructing the hive but also a fantastic addition to beauty products such as lip balm.*

Fun fact: worker bees have to **consume 5 to 6 days' worth of pollen to be able to produce beeswax.**

Benefits of Beeswax

There are many good reasons why beeswax is **such a common ingredient** in everything from food to cosmetics. Below we've listed some of the most interesting ones:

- **It's Insoluble in Water:** This makes it **amazingly useful as a sealant** for protecting wood or using it in craft projects. *It's also the reason we recommended mixing it with linseed oil to apply as a seal on your wooden beehive in chapter 4!*

- **It Burns Cleanly:** One of the best uses for beeswax is making candles because it **burns clearly and doesn't give off smoke or chemicals**. Some say that burning beeswax actually gives off negative ions, which removes "positive charge" air pollutants like dust and *cleans the air.*

- **Low Melting Point:** The melting point of beeswax is a **relatively low 63 degrees Celsius (around 145 degrees Fahrenheit)**, which means it *can be changed from a solid to a liquid very easily,* making it easy to use in a multitude of ways.

- **Chemical Components:** Beeswax is not a simple substance at all; it **includes above 250 components**, including *acids, long-chain alkanes, esters etc.* The reason beeswax is *so stable and insoluble in water* is due to it being made up of roughly 9% of Hentriacontane.

How Can I Use Beeswax?

If you have a supply of beeswax and are wondering, *"what on Earth can I do with it?"* you've come to the right place! Below we have **compiled a list of the most common uses of beeswax,** but there are many more.

Beeswax is *amazingly versatile and useful,* so don't ever just throw it away!

- Cosmetics ingredients (lip balm etc.)
- Skincare ingredients (soap etc.)
- Crafts
- Pharmaceutical uses
- Woodcare
- Waxing products
- Food production

- Official documents seal
- Candles

The list goes on! Do some further research to get more specifics on how to use it.

How to Harvest Beeswax

If you wish to extract beeswax yourself, we'll cover the best way to do it below. This method is called the **"Melt and Strain Method."**

1. Collect the "Capping" and Comb

Use a tool to **remove the caps from your frames** (just the wax that covers the combs). *Try to remove the honey* as much as possible, but some may come out naturally. *Don't worry too much about it; we'll strain the honey out later.*

Once you collect the comb, **put it in cheesecloth to strain the honey** (put it over a container to catch the honey, so you don't make a mess!)

2. Separate the Wax From the "Debris."

Tie the beeswax into a little bundle inside your cheesecloth, and **place it into a pan of simmering water.** If you have any large chunks, you can use something like a wooden spoon or stick to press them down- this *will encourage the wax to melt faster.*

Bring water to a boil, and *when the beeswax is melted completely, squeeze as much liquid out of it as possible and remove the cheesecloth from the pot* leaving behind **"wax water."**

Pour the solution into a container and **leave it to cool**. Eventually, *the wax will settle at the top, and all the dirty water will sink below it.* The wax "cake" above will still be dirty, so **we need to clean it.**

3. Clean the Wax Cake

When completely cool, **remove the solid wax cake from the liquid and melt it a second time**. Once liquid again, it *runs through a filter while still hot* to remove any remaining nasty stuff.

4. Put into a Mold

So now you *should have some nice clean wax.* Pour into any mold you have (or use it as a liquid, if required), and you're all done!

Beeswax can be used in so many amazing ways, so make sure not to neglect one of your hive's most lucrative and abundant elements.

CHAPTER 10

Beehive Care and Maintenance

"For so work the honey bees; creatures that by a rule in nature teach the act of order to a peopled kingdom.": William Shakespeare

Now we've covered all the basics for your hive and the components inside, let's look at **some general pointers and advice for both caring for and maintaining your bee colony**. Looking after your colony and maintenance of a healthy hive *go hand-in-hand.* A well-cared-for hive will house happy bees!

Firstly, the amount of maintenance you need to put into your hive can vary, but **it's important to be somewhat consistent with this time.** Like with all skills and hobbies, **you will get more out of it if you put more in.**

If you effectively maintain your beehive, the elements your bees produce will be of much higher quality. Your bees will **also be far more productive, healthy, and happy** (they'll be less likely to abscond anyway).

Most experts agree that *spring is when beehives require the most maintenance* to ensure a good honey harvest.

There are several steps a beekeeper must take when maintaining their hive.

1. General Reparations
2. Entrance Blocking
3. Excluders and Supers
4. Replace Lost Beeswax
5. Sufficient Ventilation
6. Windbreaks
7. Rain Protection/Shades
8. Woodlice and Termite Protection
9. Predator Protection

We already discussed several of these points in chapter 3 (choosing the best location for your beehive), so we'll briefly touch on them here and offer solutions.

1. General Reparations

Over time your beehive will naturally get weaker and less inhabitable for your bees; the main contributor to this is the weather which can cause issues such as *warping, rotting, cracking, and rusting.* Insects and larger animals can also cause damage to your hive.

If you can see damaged parts of your hive, they need to be repaired ASAP. If they're beyond repair, they **need to be replaced.**

If you repair and replace parts of your hive routinely, *you'll ensure that the hive can stay strong against the elements and other damaging factors.* It'll also keep your hive looking nice!

2. Entrance Blocking

Using entrance blockers is **a measure that is only really necessary in the winter.** Beekeepers limit the hive entrances to *keep heat inside and lower the burden of the bees heating it.* It also **helps to maintain adequate ventilation** and stops other nasty things from entering.

You can block your entrance by:

- Using an **entrance-reducing device** (discussed in chapter 2)
- Installing **a mesh or perforated material over the entrance** with holes big enough to allow your bees through.
- **Blocking some of the hive's multiple entrances** with pieces of wood.

3. Excluders and Supers

As we discussed in chapter 2, the queen excluder is a layer that separates the brood from the comb, preventing the queen from laying eggs where she shouldn't. Supers are *the space that bees actually fill with honey when their honeycomb or brood combs are full.*

To help you keep your hive in tip-top working condition, it's **a lot easier to use a queen excluder.** So install one if you haven't already.

Installing extra supers will also keep your hive working well, giving **your bees the extra storage they need during their busy season** (spring to summer).

4. Replace Lost Beeswax

We touched on beeswax for a whole chapter in chapter 6, so **we should know by now how important it is.** Beeswax is *what bees use to line the hive interior to make it stronger and more comfortable,* as well as make combs to store their honey. So **if any of it is broken or lost, it's not good.**

It's a pretty common situation that beeswax will get lost when honey is harvested, as the beekeeper can easily break it off accidentally when prying open their hive or removing frames. Use a hive tool to prevent yourself from doing this, but also **make sure you try to reattach any wax you break off if possible.**

If you need to replace large chunks of wax, you can *use excess wax from another hive* if you have it or buy **natural replacement beeswax** from a store.

5. Sufficient Ventilation

We've touched on why ventilation is so important before: **there shouldn't be too much or too little**. If the hive is over or under-ventilated, it *can cause significant damage to the interior.*

If the hive is poorly ventilated, **water or even ice can form inside, harming the structure** and the bees themselves. *Lack of ventilation can also cause the hive to overheat,* which can also cause damage as well as cause the bees discomfort. When overheating, you'll **see your bees exhibit certain behaviors, such as bearding (see photo) or fanning.**

6. Windbreaks

Strong winds can **wreak havoc on beehives**. Not only can it *push moist or cold air into the hive cavity, but it can also cause the whole thing to topple over,* which **will destroy a lot of your bee's hard work.**

Installing a windbreaker is a good idea to protect your hive from excessive wind. It *can be natural (trees, shrubs, etc.) or artificial* (a fence, sheet of material, etc.).

Make sure to **check where the wind typically blows from** in your local area.

7. Rain Protection/Shade

As we mentioned before, the weather can be a huge problem for your hive. *Rainwater, or moisture of any kind, can damage the hive and disturb your bees greatly,* as well as possibly kill them. *Excessive direct sunlight* can sadly have the same effect.

- To protect your hive from rain, it's **a good idea to use some kind of outer cover or slanted cover** to allow the rain to roll off it. Something fashioned from plastic or metal would be good.
- To shade the hive from direct sun, you can **either fashion something to provide shade or choose your hive's location based on its sun exposure.**

If you opt for using a rain cover, then **make sure you don't leave it on constantly, as it can affect the hive being ventilated efficiently.** If excessive water does somehow make its way into your hive, *position your hive on a slight incline to allow the liquid to drain out.*

8. Woodlice and Termite Protection

Pests such as woodlice and termites are a nightmare for beekeepers. As most of us opt for using wood to make our beehives, **these creatures can easily feed on your hive and gradually destroy it.** Woodlice and termites are *particularly ruthless during the drier months* and can easily lurk inside old or rotten wood.

- To limit these pests, you can *apply liquid insecticides, baits, or soil treatment* (get advice from your local beekeepers for the best options and **make sure these methods will not harm your bees before use.**)

- You can also prevent them by *removing the surrounding foliage around your apiary.*

9. Predator Protection

Several animals are likely to cause issues for your hive, including **bears, mice, skunks, raccoons,** etc. Let's look at each of these in detail and provide some solutions.

- **Bears** love to destroy hives and eat honeycomb. If bears are commonly found where you live, you can deter them by *putting a strong fence/perimeter around your hive.*
- **Mice** are infamous for *building nests in beehives,* which can cause you and your bees a plethora of problems. You *can deter mice by installing a mouse guard* near your hive entrance.

- **Mice and skunks** also *tend to dig holes in hives*, destroying the bee's comb and making *the hive generally uninhabitable*. To prevent skunks, the best way is to *make sure your hive is on a stand that is elevated sufficiently*.

- **Raccoons** can also be a major source of damage to your beehive. They *often enter beehives through the lid to get inside*, so you can prevent this by *adding some kind of weight or lock to your hive's lid/roof*.

CONCLUSION

And that **covers all the basic things you need to know to start your bee apiary!**

In this book, we've covered a variety of useful topics, including; a background on beekeeping, why to keep bees, what you need to get started, how to find bees, what a beehive includes, types of beehives, how to choose the perfect beehive location, how to build a beehive, how to harvest honey and beeswax, and finally how to care for your bee colony.

Beekeeping is a **complex and highly intricate subject** that is **ever-changing**, so the best piece of advice for any new beekeeper is to **get dive in and never stop learning!** There are tons of materials out there available for people interested in beekeeping, and so much to learn. And don't forget to find some beekeeping friends along the way. What you can learn from them will be truly fascinating.

Good luck!

Made in the USA
Columbia, SC
04 November 2023

25462558R00054